When
Dinosaurs Walked

Written by Andrew Chaikin

Illustrated by Patricia Wynne

World Book, Inc.
a Scott Fetzer company
Chicago

When Dinosaurs Walked

World Book, Inc.
233 N. Michigan Avenue
Chicago, IL 60601

ISBN 0-7166-1607-6 ISBN 0-7166-1647-5 (set)
Library of Congress Control Number: 2003116751

Printed in Malaysia
2 3 4 5 6 7 8 9 08 07 06

For information about other World Book publications, visit our
Web site **http://www.worldbook.com** or call **1-800-WORLDBK
(967-5325).** For information about sales to schools and libraries,
call **1-800-975-3250 (United States); 1-800-837-5365 (Canada).**

Cover design by Rosa Cabrera
Book design by Mary-Ann Lupa

Once, long ago, giant animals could make the ground shake when they walked. Flying reptiles soared through the air. Some great beasts had teeth longer than your hand. Who were these creatures? Dinosaurs, of course—and other reptiles! Millions of years ago, they ruled the earth.

When reptiles ruled, the earth was different. It may have been warmer and wetter than it is today. There were no people back then, but dinosaurs were all around. What were the dinosaurs like? How do we know about them?

Some of their teeth, bones, and eggs have been found inside layers of rock. These things are called fossils. Scientists use fossils as clues to figure out what the dinosaurs were like. Let's step back into the days of the dinosaurs.

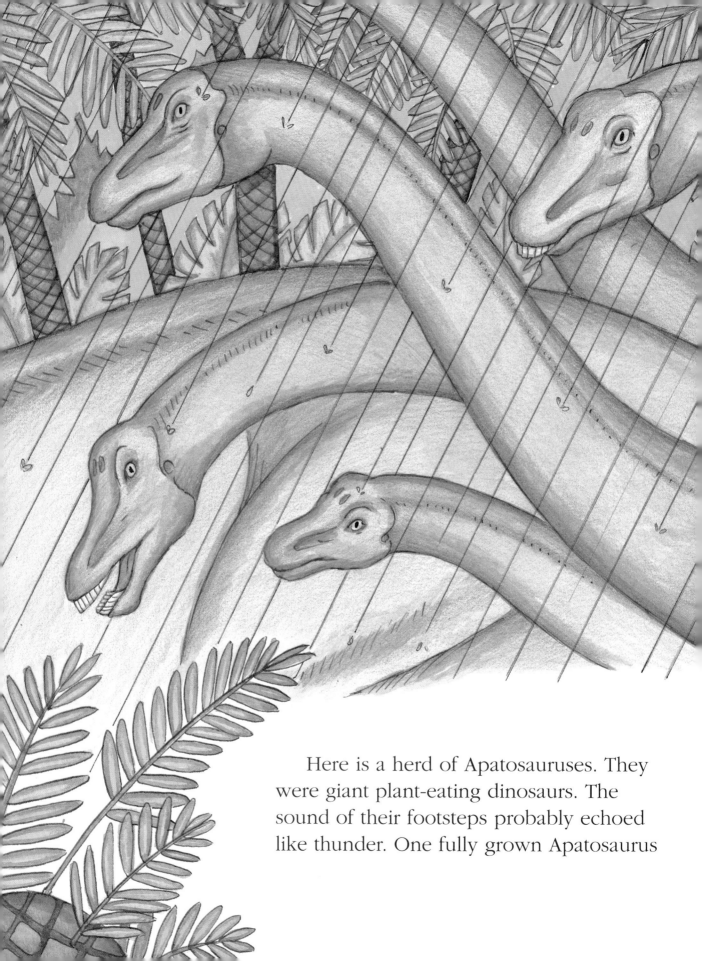

Here is a herd of Apatosauruses. They were giant plant-eating dinosaurs. The sound of their footsteps probably echoed like thunder. One fully grown Apatosaurus

Apatosaurus
(ap uh toh SAWR uhs)

could weigh more than five elephants. Its
neck was so long that it could reach up and
bite the leaves off the tallest of trees. Can
you imagine anything bigger?

7

A few years ago, a scientist discovered some fossils in the western United States. It's not certain that all of the bones from this find came from the same dinosaur, but if they did, this animal would be the largest dinosaur ever found.

Named Ultrasauros because of its great size, this dinosaur could have been three times heavier than Apatosaurus and nearly twice as tall. Ultrasauros was a plant eater, and it probably traveled in herds looking for food to eat from the tallest trees.

Ultrasauros
(uhl truh SAWR ohs)

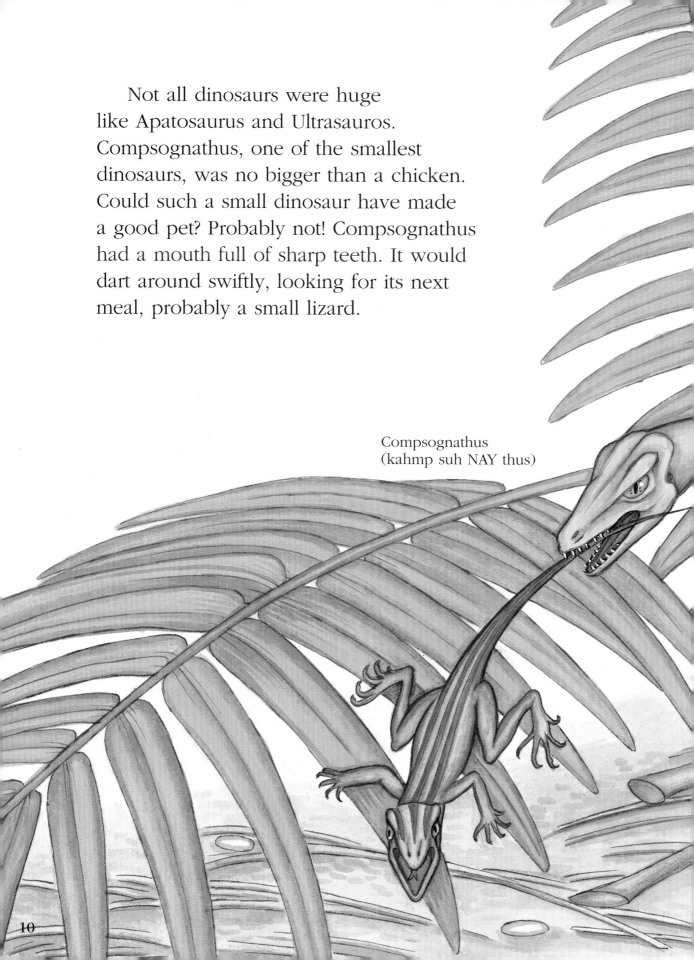

Not all dinosaurs were huge like Apatosaurus and Ultrasauros. Compsognathus, one of the smallest dinosaurs, was no bigger than a chicken. Could such a small dinosaur have made a good pet? Probably not! Compsognathus had a mouth full of sharp teeth. It would dart around swiftly, looking for its next meal, probably a small lizard.

Compsognathus
(kahmp suh NAY thus)

How do we know which dinosaurs ate plants and which ate other animals? Their teeth give a clue. Scientists have been able to tell what different dinosaurs ate by studying fossils of their teeth.

Look at the teeth of Apatosaurus. They are flat on the ends and shaped like pegs, like the teeth of a cow. Since we know that cows eat plants, Apatosaurus probably did, also.

The teeth of Allosaurus are sharp, like a lion's. Lions are meat-eaters. What do you think Allosaurus ate?

Today, on the plains of Africa, an unlucky giraffe may end up as dinner for a hungry lion. In the time of the dinosaurs, hungry meat-eaters like Allosaurus may have hunted plant-eaters like Apatosaurus. The big plant-eater was probably too slow to run away.

How do we know this? Scientists found the bones of an Apatosaurus next to the bones of an Allosaurus. The Allosaurus' teeth marks could still be seen in the Apatosaurus' tail. That Apatosaurus became dinner for Allosaurus.

Allosaurus
(al uh SAWR uhs)

Tyrannosaurus
(tih RAN uh sawr uhs)

One dinosaur was perhaps the fiercest beast of all time. Do you know which dinosaur it was? Tyrannosaurus rex, of course. Imagine three tall people today standing on top of one another. That's about as tall as Tyrannosaurus, who also had a mouth full of sharp, jagged teeth and hooklike claws on its hands and feet.

How could the plant-eaters protect themselves from Tyrannosaurus? Some couldn't. But the small, fast ones could run away. And other dinosaurs had armor. Look at Triceratops' three horns and that bony shield around its neck. How do you think Triceratops protected itself?

Triceratops
(try SEHR uh tahps)

Ankylosaurus was a dinosaur with a different kind of protection. Its body was covered with hard, bony knobs and spikes. An ankylosaur's tail ended in a bony club that it could use like a weapon. One swing of that clubbed tail could have been enough to scare off most enemies.

Ankylosaurus
(an KY luh sawr uhs)

Elasmosaurus
(ih laz muh SAWR uhs)

While dinosaurs walked the land, other reptiles lived in the seas of long ago.

Look at Elasmosaurus. This creature used its long neck to lunge at fast-moving fish. Its mouth was full of sharp teeth.

Mosasaurus looked a little like a crocodile, but instead of feet, it had flippers for swimming. Its long, powerful tail helped guide it through the water.

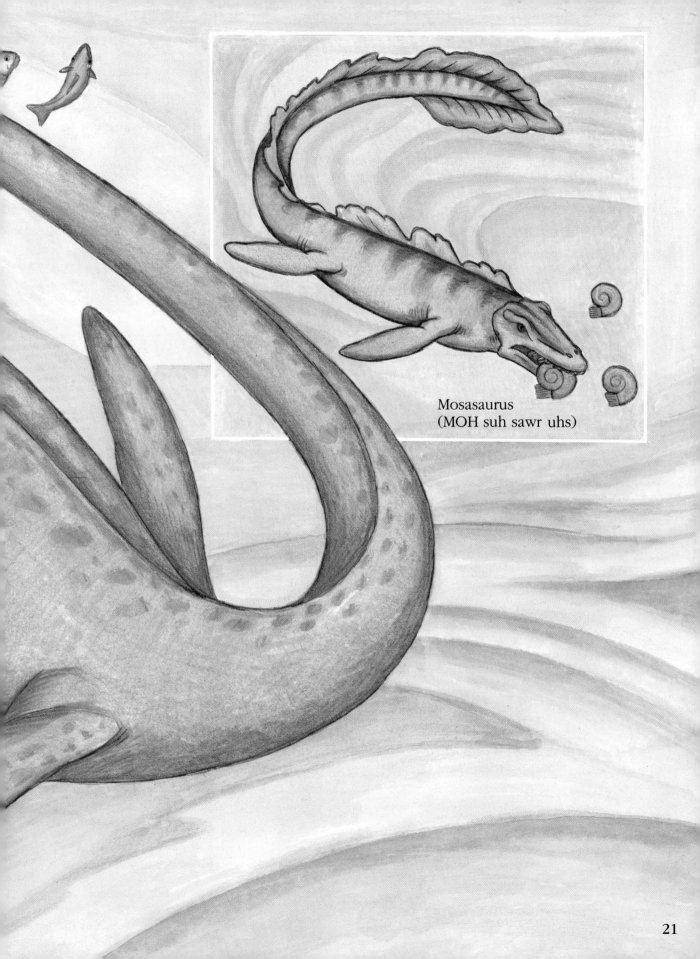

Mosasaurus
(MOH suh sawr uhs)

Back when the dinosaurs walked the
land, there were different kinds of flying
reptiles, too. Pteranodon had a body about
the size of a turkey, but its wingspan was
immense—about 26 feet. That's about as
much distance as four tall people lying head
to foot! Can you imagine such a creature,
swooping down to the water to catch fish?

And then there was the smaller
Pterodactylus, no bigger than a robin.
With its leathery wings, do you think
Pterodactylus looks something like a bat?
This reptile probably snapped up insects
with its long jaws.

Pteranodon
(tehr AN uh dahn)

22

Pterodactylus
(tehr uh DAK
tuh luhs)

For a time, another creature shared the skies with the flying reptiles. Here is Archaeopteryx. In some ways it was like the reptiles, because it had teeth. But Archaeopteryx was covered with feathers—unlike any dinosaur or other reptile. Doesn't Archaeopteryx look like a bird? Scientists call it the first known bird.

Archaeopteryx
(ahr kee AHP tuhr ihks)

Today, no dinosaurs shake the ground as they walk. No flying reptiles soar. These creatures, and others, are gone. What happened to them? Some scientists think that a meteorite—a huge chunk of rock from space—crashed into the earth. The crash might have kicked up a thick cloud of dust. The dust might have blocked the sun's light and heat.

Other scientists think that dinosaurs died off slowly, over a long period of time. They think that the earth was growing colder and the dinosaurs could not live in the new climate.

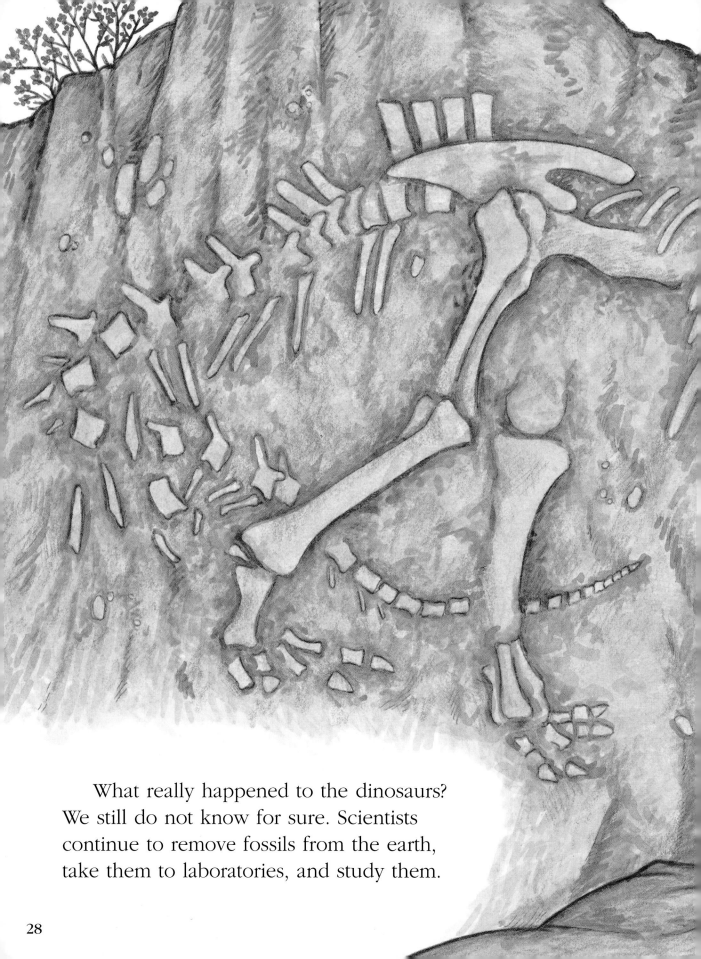

What really happened to the dinosaurs? We still do not know for sure. Scientists continue to remove fossils from the earth, take them to laboratories, and study them.

What will they find out? Every discovery tells us something. Maybe the bones tell of a new kind of early reptile. Maybe they tell us more about how the dinosaurs lived and what happened to them. There is still so much to learn about those long-ago days when dinosaurs walked the earth.

Is it an ancient bird, a dinosaur, a flying reptile, or a marine reptile?

Is it a meat-eating dinosaur or a plant-eating dinosaur?

More About Dinosaurs

When the dinosaurs first evolved, the continents were not as we know them today. More than 200 million years ago there was one "super continent," which scientists have named Pangaea. Later, this continent broke apart—first two large continents were formed, but eventually the continents we are familiar with emerged. We find dinosaur fossils on every modern continent.

For many years, scientists assumed dinosaurs, like modern reptiles, were cold-blooded. That would probably have meant they were slow-moving beasts. Today, most scientists believe that some dinosaurs were warm-blooded like mammals and were capable of running and moving quite quickly.

Most dinosaurs probably laid eggs like modern reptiles. But unlike reptiles, at least some dinosaurs cared for their young the way birds do. They kept nests and brought back food for the babies to eat. Fossil nests with eggs and baby dinosaurs have been found in the western United States.